P9-CQV-060

Kevin Durant

By Jeff Savage

AMAZING ATHLETES

Lerner Publications Company • Minneapolis

Lerner Publications Company
A division of Lerner Publishing Group, Inc.
241 First Avenue North
Minneapolis, MN 55401 U.S.A.

Website address: www.lernerbooks.com

Library of Congress Cataloging-in-Publication Data

Savage, Jeff, 1961–
    Kevin Durant / by Jeff Savage.
       p.   cm. — (Amazing athletes)
    Includes index.
    ISBN 978–0–7613–7671–2 (lib. bdg. : alk. paper)
    1. Durant, Kevin, 1988– —Juvenile literature. 2. Basketball players—United States—Biography—Juvenile literature. 3. Oklahoma City Thunder (Basketball team)—Juvenile literature. I. Title.
GV884.D868S38 2012
796.323092—dc22 [B]   2011011397

Manufactured in the United States of America
1 – BP – 7/15/11

TABLE OF CONTENTS

Kevin Durant takes a shot.

SWEET SPOT

Kevin Durant grabbed the pass from Pau Gasol. Kevin rose up and took a **three-point shot**. Swish!

Kevin was playing in the 2011 National Basketball Association (NBA) **All-Star Game**. A sold-out crowd at the Staples Center in Los Angeles was watching Kevin put on a show.

The Western **Conference** was ahead of the Eastern Conference in the second quarter. Kevin made a pair of **free throws** for the West to stretch the lead. Moments later, Chris Paul passed the basketball to Kevin near the basket. Eastern players Dwight Howard and Amar'e Stoudemire came toward him. Kevin flicked in a **jumper** from 13 feet away. "My sweet spot," Kevin calls it. Kevin's basket gave the West a 12-point halftime lead.

Kevin stays focused during the All-Star Game.

Kevin does not crave attention. But with 15 points in the first half of the All-Star Game, he was in the spotlight. Kevin is the beanpole-thin shooting star of the Oklahoma City Thunder.

Basketball is a team sport. Kevin puts the team first. "I'll play all five positions if my team needs me to," he says.

His arms are nearly as long as broomsticks. A year earlier, as a baby-faced 21-year-old, he became the youngest player ever to lead the NBA in scoring.

The secret to Kevin's success is simple. "Work harder than your opponent," he says. Fans respect him. They cast more than 1.7 million votes for Kevin to play in the All-Star Game. "I really appreciate the fans voting for me," he said. "I've put in a lot of hard work and it shows that I've been doing things the right way."

Kevin made more great plays in the second half. He outjumped Dwight Howard to throw down a two-hand **slam dunk**. Later, Kevin soared past Miami Heat star LeBron James for another dunk!

Kevin takes the ball to the basket.

The East rallied to get within two points with 2:18 left in the game. Kevin's jumper made the lead four points. Then he took a pass from Kobe Bryant and buried a three-pointer! The West won the game, 148–143.

The All-Star Game Most Valuable Player (MVP) award went to Bryant. It could have easily gone to Kevin, who finished with 34 points. "It was an honor to be voted to play," said Kevin. "I'm just going to try to continue to get better every day as a person and as a player."

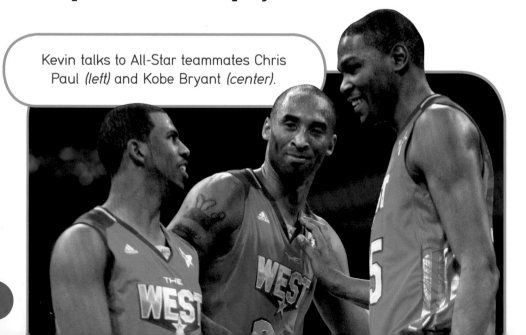

Kevin talks to All-Star teammates Chris Paul *(left)* and Kobe Bryant *(center)*.

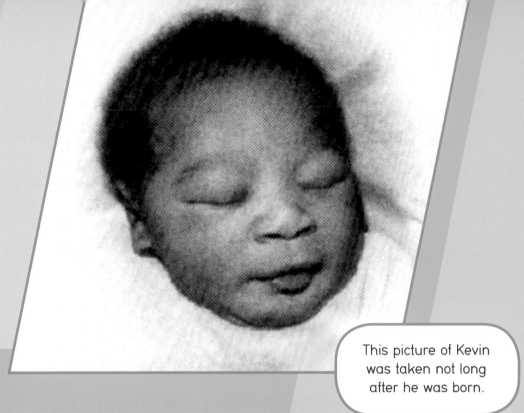

This picture of Kevin was taken not long after he was born.

WORKING HARD

Kevin Wayne Durant was born September 29, 1988, in Suitland, Maryland. Wanda, his mother, was a postal worker. His father, Wayne, was a police officer. His grandmother, Barbara Davis, also helped raise Kevin. He had two brothers, Anthony and Rayvonne, and one sister, Briana.

Kevin rode the bus to school, where he earned good grades. But he learned his most important lesson at home. "My mother taught me to always work hard," he said. "She's been working hard her whole life."

Kevin joined his first youth basketball team in 1997 at the age of nine. Charles Craig coached the PG Jaguars. One of Kevin's teammates was Michael Beasley. Kevin and Michael became best friends. Beasley later became a star for the Minnesota Timberwolves. The Jaguars won several championships.

Kevin was 10 when he began to get serious about basketball. Taras Brown was a coach at the local activities center. He agreed to help Kevin.

Kevin worked hard for Coach Brown. Kevin ran up hills. On the gym floor, he lay on his back and held a heavy ball above his head. "I was supposed to hold it there for an hour," Kevin said. "An hour!"

Before long, Kevin's arms would ache. "But I know it's those types of drills that made me what I am today," he said.

Kevin carried a basketball with him everywhere. His friends teased him because his T-shirts were marked with basketball prints. "I was always in the gym," he said. "People would look at me crazy because I spent so much time there."

Kevin was a junior in high school when tragedy struck. Kevin learned that Charles Craig, his first youth coach, had been murdered. Craig was only 35 years old. To honor his coach, Kevin wore jersey number 35 at the University of Texas. He also wears number 35 with the Thunder.

The practice paid off. In 2004, Kevin starred as a high school junior at Oak Hill Academy. At a height of six feet seven, Kevin dominated near the basket. He could also shoot from long range.

For his senior season, Kevin transferred to Montrose Christian High in Rockville, Maryland. He grew two more inches to his current height of six feet nine. He won All-America honors as one of the best high school basketball players in the country.

Kevin (right) and Chase Budinger (left) were named co-MVPs of the McDonald's All-American High School Basketball Game in 2006.

... during his first ... y of Texas in 2006.

ON... ...ME

Kevin ... ...lleges. He got letter... ...Mike Krzyzewski of Duke Un... ...Carolina and Roy Williams of North Carolina. Kevin said it "felt good" to be wanted. He chose to attend the University of Texas.

There were many questions for the 2006–2007 Texas Longhorns basketball team. The Longhorns play in the Big 12 Conference. Kevin was one of four freshman **starters**. Were these youngsters ready for big-time college basketball?

Kevin gave an immediate answer. In his team's first game, he scored 20 points to lead the Longhorns to a 103–44 win over Alcorn State. In each of his next six games, Kevin scored even more points! Texas coach Rick Barnes allowed Kevin to play freely. "He's a once-in-a-lifetime guy," said the coach.

Coach Rick Barnes congratulates Kevin at the end of a game in 2007.

Kevin scored 37 points against the University of Colorado. Then he scored 37 more against Oklahoma State. He had his best game yet at Texas Tech, with 37 points and 23 rebounds.

Kevin led Texas to the Big 12 Tournament title game against the University of Kansas. He scored 37 points again, but the Longhorns lost the game. Even though his team came up short, Kevin was named tournament MVP.

Kevin lays the ball in the hoop during the 2007 Big 12 Conference tournament.

The Longhorns played in the 2007 National Collegiate Athletic Association (NCAA) Tournament. They beat New Mexico State, 79–67. Texas faced the University of Southern California (USC) in their second game. Kevin did all he could by scoring 30 points. But the Longhorns lost, 87–68. Their season was over.

Kevin won an armful of awards after the 2006–2007 season. He became the first freshman ever to be named Associated Press National Player of the Year. Coach Barnes was

Kevin hugs his father after being named the Associated Press National Player of the Year in 2007.

proud of Kevin. "He carried a very young team but never looked at it that way," the coach said after the season. "He has such a great feel for the game."

Kevin was still a teenager. But he knew he was ready to play in the NBA. He declared himself **eligible** for the **draft**.

The 2007 NBA draft was held on June 28. Kevin was the second player chosen. The Seattle SuperSonics thought Kevin could be their **franchise** player.

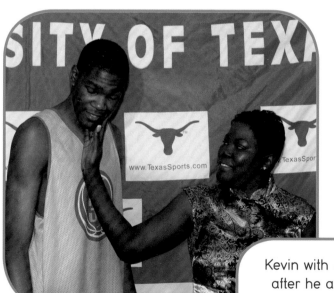

Kevin with his mother in 2007 after he announced that he was leaving Texas for the NBA.

Kevin looks happy after being drafted by the Seattle SuperSonics.

TEEN SENSATION

In 2007 Kevin signed a **contract** with Seattle worth millions of dollars. Then he signed **endorsement** deals. Nike paid him $60 million to **sponsor** their company for the next seven years. EA Sports and Gatorade paid him $20 million more. Kevin was rich, and he was still only 19 years old!

Kevin and his mother moved into a nice house in Seattle. Neighborhood children often came over to play video games with Kevin. "Sometimes they bring him cookies," said his mother.

The SuperSonics showed Kevin how to gain weight and strength. "I'm supposed to eat the same stuff, only more of it," Kevin said. "Four eggs instead of two. Four pieces of baked chicken instead of two. But it's going to be lifting weights and normal growth that will really put the weight on."

Kevin's mother holds up her son's new SuperSonics jersey in 2007.

Kevin played his first pro game on Halloween night against the Denver Nuggets. He wanted to ask Nuggets star Carmelo Anthony for his autograph. But he kept quiet. "I was nervous," Kevin said, "but the butterflies went away." Kevin scored 18 points, but his team lost.

The SuperSonics played the following night against the Phoenix Suns. Before the game, two-time NBA MVP Steve Nash said hello to Kevin as he walked by. "I couldn't believe he knew my name!" Kevin said.

Kevin was very popular with the fans in Seattle.

Kevin shoots the game-winning three-pointer against the Atlanta Hawks.

Despite Kevin's efforts, his team lost their next two games. "We will get better," Kevin said.

In mid-November, Kevin made his first game-winning shot—a three-pointer to beat the Atlanta Hawks in **double overtime**! Later that month, he scored 35 points to help beat the Indiana Pacers. Kevin was named NBA Rookie of the Month for November. He was unstoppable. He won the award again in December, January, March, and April.

In the final game of the 2007–2008 season, Kevin scored 42 points against the Golden State Warriors. Still just 19 years old, Kevin was the youngest player ever to score so many points in the NBA. He became just the third teenager in NBA history to average over 20 points per game for a full season. He was an easy choice as Rookie of the Year.

When the season ended, the SuperSonics left Seattle. The team moved to Oklahoma City. Their new nickname was the Thunder.

Kevin poses with his Rookie of the Year trophy in 2008.

Kevin showed up for practice each day early and stayed late. Kevin was working hard, but his teammates weren't much help. The Thunder started the 2008–2009 season with a record of 3–29. Kevin stayed positive. "The fans have been with me every night,"

Kevin dunks the ball during a 2009 game against the Los Angeles Lakers.

he said. "What more can you ask for?"

The Thunder finished the season with just 23 wins in 82 games. "I've learned what it feels like to lose," Kevin said. "But in the end, that is just going to make winning that much better."

Kevin and Russell Westbrook *(left)* played
well together in Oklahoma City.

WINNING TIME

Every NBA star needs a **sidekick** for his team to
be great. While the Thunder were losing, Kevin
learned to play well with fast **point guard**
Russell Westbrook. In 2009–2010, they became
a dynamic duo.

Opponents double-teamed Kevin by putting
a **defender** in front of him and another behind.

Kevin passed to Westbrook for open shots. The Thunder started winning. Sellout crowds filled Ford Center in Oklahoma City to see the exciting pair.

The Thunder won 50 games! They made the **playoffs**. Oklahoma City faced the powerful Los Angeles Lakers in a best-of-seven series. The Thunder lost the first two games in Los Angeles. Kevin scored 29 points in Game 3 and 22 more in Game 4 to lead Oklahoma City to a pair of victories. The series was tied. The Thunder lost the next game. One more loss would end their season.

A big crowd watches a Thunder game in Oklahoma City.

Kevin *(left)* closely watches Lakers star Kobe Bryant in Game 6.

Game 6 was at the Ford Center. Kevin scored 26 points to lead his team. It wasn't enough. The Lakers won the game, 95–94. Afterward, the crowd stood and applauded the hometown team for a great effort.

Kevin acted like a **veteran**. It was hard to believe he was just 21 years old. He led the NBA in scoring to become the youngest player ever to win the scoring title. He finished second in MVP voting to LeBron James.

The Thunder adored Kevin. They gave him a five-year **extension** on his contract for $85 million. Kevin repaid the Thunder in 2010–2011 with more great performances. He beat the New York Knicks with a three-pointer in the final seconds of the game. He scored 47 points against the Minnesota Timberwolves, including 16 in a row in the fourth quarter! Coaches marvel at how Kevin acts. "You never see Durant pumping his chest or saying 'Look at what I just did,'" said San Antonio Spurs coach Gregg Popovich.

Kevin goes to the basket during a 2011 game against the Minnesota Timberwolves. Kevin's grade school teammate Michael Beasley is the defender.

Kevin has a good time with the crowd during a basketball camp for kids in Oklahoma City in 2010.

Kevin says he owes his success to his childhood. That is when he learned the value of hard work. "I know that the hard work got me here," he admits. "Hard work beats talent when talent fails to work hard. The day I stop working hard, this can all go away. I will always work hard."

Selected Career Highlights

2010–2011   Named International Basketball Federation World Championship MVP
Led Thunder to the playoffs
Scored 34 points in NBA All-Star Game

2009–2010   Led Thunder to the playoffs
Was youngest player to win NBA scoring title
Finished second in NBA MVP Award voting
Played in first NBA All-Star Game

2008–2009   Led Thunder in scoring with an average of 25.3 points per game
Named MVP of Rookie/Sophomore T-Mobile Challenge after scoring record 46 points
Won first-ever H-O-R-S-E competition at All-Star Game

2007–2008   Voted NBA Rookie of the Year
Named NBA Rookie of the Month five times
Led all rookies in scoring
Broke Seattle SuperSonics all-time rookie season scoring record

2006–2007   Led University of Texas to NCAA Tournament
Named Big 12 Player of the Year
Awarded the Oscar Robertson Trophy
Awarded the Adolph Rupp Trophy
Named Naismith Player of the Year
Won the John R. Wooden Award
Voted Associated Press National Player of the Year
Selected second overall in NBA Draft

2005–2006   Named McDonald's High School All-American
Named co-MVP of the McDonald's All-American High School Basketball Game

Glossary

All-Star Game: a game held midway through the NBA season featuring the best players in each conference

conference: in the NBA, one of the two groups of teams. The groups are the Western Conference and the Eastern Conference. In college, one of many groups of teams, such as the Big 12 Conference and the Atlantic Coast Conference.

contract: a deal signed by a player and a team that states the amount of money the player is paid and the number of years he plays

defender: a player whose job it is to stop the other team from scoring

double overtime: a second period of extra time played to decide the winner of a game. Double overtime is played if the score is still tied after a first overtime.

draft: a yearly event in which teams take turns choosing new players from a group

eligible: available to be chosen in the draft

endorsement: a deal in which a person is paid to represent a company and its products

extension: more years added to a contract to make the contract last longer

franchise: in sports, the player most valuable to a team and its future

free throws: one-point shots taken from behind the free-throw line

jumper: jump shot, a shot in which the player shoots the ball toward the basket while jumping in the air

playoffs: a series of games held every year to decide a champion

point guard: the player on a basketball team who is responsible for running the team's scoring plays. Point guards are skilled at dribbling and passing.

recruited: encouraged to join a college basketball team

sidekick: a supporting player

slam dunk: when a player slams the basketball through the basket

sponsor: to represent a company and its products

starters: players who are on the court at the beginning of a basketball game

three-point shot: a basketball shot taken from long-range that is worth three points

veteran: a player with experience

Further Reading & Websites

Kennedy, Mike, and Mark Stewart. *Swish: The Quest for Basketball's Perfect Shot*. Minneapolis: Millbrook Press, 2009.

Ladewski, Paul. *Megastars 2010*. New York: Scholastic, 2011.

Savage, Jeff. *Dwight Howard*. Minneapolis: Lerner Publications Company, 2011.

Savage, Jeff. *Kobe Bryant*. Minneapolis: Lerner Publications Company, 2011.

Savage, Jeff. *Steve Nash*. Minneapolis: Lerner Publications Company, 2007.

Kevin's Official Site
http://www.kevindurant35.com
Kevin's personal website includes a biography, a blog, tweets, photos, and the latest news about Kevin and the Thunder.

Oklahoma City Thunder: The Official Site
http://www.nba.com/thunder
The official website of the Oklahoma City Thunder includes the team schedule and game results, late-breaking news, biographies of players like Kevin Durant, and much more.

Sports Illustrated Kids
http://www.sikids.com
The *Sports Illustrated Kids* website covers all sports, including basketball.

Index

Photo Acknowledgments

The images in this book are used with the permission of: © Icon Sports Media, p. 4; © Mark Ralston/AFP/Getty Images, p. 6; © Lucy Nicholson/Getty Images, p. 7; © Michael Goulding/The Orange County Register/ZUMA Press, p. 8; Seth Poppel Yearbook Library, p. 9; AP Photo/Denis Poroy, p. 12; AP Photo/Harry Cabluck, p. 13; AP Photo/LM Otero, p. 14; © Jamie Squire/Getty Images, p. 15; AP Photo/John Bazemore, p. 16; AP Photo/Jack Plunkett, p. 17; AP Photo/Kathy Willens, p. 18; AP Photo/John Froschauer, p. 19; © Doug Pensinger/Getty Images, p. 20; © Kevin C. Cox/Getty Images, p. 21; AP Photo/Ted S. Warren, p. 22; AP Photo/Sue Ogrocki, p. 23; AP Photo/David Zalubowski, p. 24; © J.P. Wilson/Bloomberg via Getty Images, p. 25; AP Photo/Alonzo Adams, p. 26; AP Photo/Jim Mone, p. 27; AP Photo/The Oklahoman, Mitchell Alcala, p. 28; © Chris Graythen/Getty Images, p. 29.

Front cover: © Harry How/Getty Images.

Main body text set in Caecilia LT std 55 Roman 16/28. Typeface provided by Linotype AG.